INSIGHT PUBLICA®

INSIGHT PUBLICA®
Nadakkave, Kozhikode, Kerala, India
+91 4954020666 | +91 9400737475
www.insightpublica.com
e-mail: insightpublica@gmail.com
The Soulful Melodies
Sidharth PK
(English Poems)
First Edition: August 2020

ISBN 978-81-947032-0-4

The Soulful Melodies

SIDHARTH PK

INSIGHT PUBLICA®

Born in Palakkad on August 10th 1998, Sidharth pk is a graduate in sociology, from Sacred Heart college, Thevara. He is a well versed quizzer as well as avid reader especially history, philosophy and literature. His writings included poetry, short stories and essays. His poems had appeared in newspapers and leading magazines. Sidharth has participated and won prizes in various intercollegiate competitions. His literary tastes included Byronic poetry, Shelley, John Keats and Robert Frost.

Sidharth is a multi talented persona and his talents varies from writing poetry, academics, quiz master and public speaking.

SIDHARTH PK

Forward

As the title, so is the content. Soulful Melodies. The young author appears to reveal a very tender heart, seeking love and enamoured by beauty. Believe it is natural for the youth to be full of love and associate that with the beauty of the youth. The author nimbly shifting from human love to the loveable universe and to the earth and the life on it and back to human love...

Both beauty and youth will pass by, but what can stay and should stay is love that will transcend time, age, appearances, distance and differences. Poet Mahadevi Varma describes this in one of her romantic poems beautifully.

I hope that the youth of today will find lasting love in spite of the brokenness involved in being in love.

J Prasant CMI
Principal
Sacred Heart College
Thevara.

Acknowledgements

I hereby express my deep gratitude to many who helped me in realising this dream come true. A special thanks to Dilip uncle and Biju uncle for their tremendous encouragement and support rendered to me in the initial stage of my writing. I'm overwhelmed by the immense support and kind help that I got from Fr Prasant Palakkilpaly , principal sacred heart college, thevara. I also extent my sincere thanks to Fr Xavier joy, Fr joby manamanl, Fr Sabu , Fr Tomason, Dr Rajesh Manayil sir for their inspiring and immense support. Last, but not the least, I also take the opportunity to thank all my well wishers in this hour, thank you all.

Preface

Poetry is that form of an art which allows a writer to put his heart on paper. It is the most comprised form of literature. This book contains poems penned by me since childhood. I want to say that I'm a poet by experience and my poems represent a lover's lost love, a child's wavering dream, the anguish and tears of faded love. Many poets have inspired me, including P b Shelley, Lord Byron, Keats and Pablo Neurdo. Their works have left a lasting impression upon me. This book is an anthology of my verse collection. The cherished dreams blossoms into my poetry.

Poems

Lines Addressed to an Indian Beauty

Living miles away,
I still can feel you
The tenderness of your lips
Music of your heart,
Overflowing like melodious note.
Living miles away,
I still can see you
In my soul
Deep love for you
My dear girl

Living miles away,
I still can sense you
The softness of your touch
That sparked my core,
Endearing my sweet.
Living miles away,
Mountains divide us
But I claim
My darling
Never feel we are miles apart...

Remember Femi, Remember Femi

The Aegean breeze that blows,
Gives me thoughts of relish love
Remembrance, the very word
Fills me with anguish
For my love was feverish,
Dead and gone.
Thy looks captured my imagination,
Thee forever remain beautiful
As the age chills passion in me
Thy voice like music to my ears
Sweeten in ripened love,
Remember Femi, I still love you.
The pleasure of human sin,
Dark page in my book
Wolves will find a prey
Night blooming darker
Let me go and sleep,
And expire in mystery.

My First Love

A mist of passion,
Weeping soul
And half broken hearted
My first love
Can I forget it?
The love that time
Has mortal washed away
Sweetly the days
That I recall,
Can I forget thee?
The pain and sorrow,
Of our parted love
Is not for tomorrow
Like the wind that kiss the tree
I not kiss thou?
The first love has vanished,
Away into mystery
Recollections of a faded romance
Saddest thoughts carry away me,
To tears and anguish.

Morning Melody

Rise and shine, my lord
Rise and shine, O my lord,
Sings the sweet robin
Roses are in full bloom
Their sister daisies too
Petals fresh and fragrant.
Rise and shine, my lord
Rise and shine, O my lord,
Sings the heavenly angel
Sun has awoken
His lovely offspring earth,
Light here all surrounds.
Rise and shine, my lord
Rise and shine, O my lord
Harbingers of dawn chant
In a beautiful cadence
Man is already about,
Seeking his daily bread.

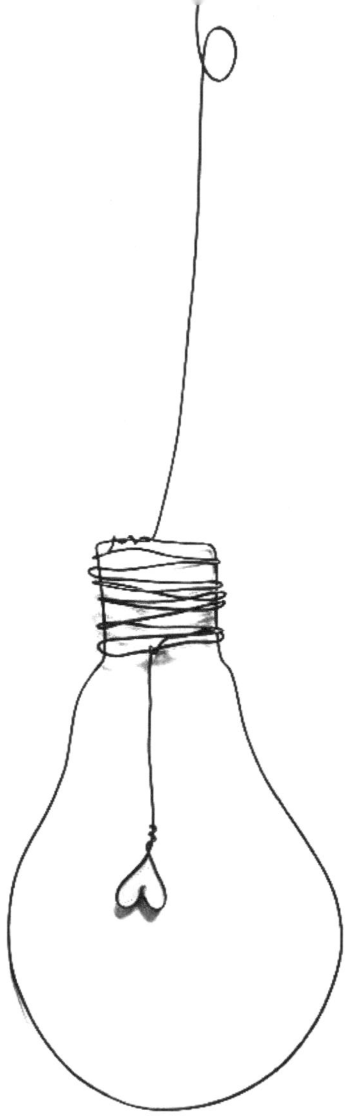

O Heavenly Bells

O Heavenly bells,
I hear them ring
In soft poignant verses
Like angel's sweet throated cadence
At an age seventeen and prime.
O Heavenly Bells,
I hear them ring
Disharmonious whimpers upon tender ears
Echoing from Heaven's every corner
Reflecting earth's silent and agonizing tears.

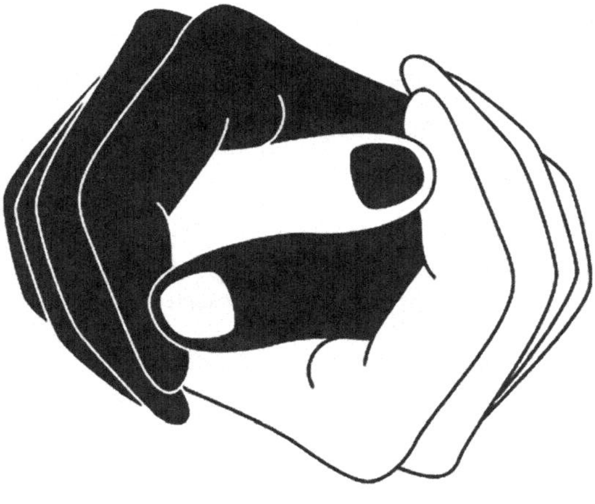

On Love

Sweet rain showers brings love,
And falls on a flowing dove
A dewy rose calls the bee
O to suck honey from thee.
An infant upon her sweet breast sleeps,
A lover on his lass's grave weeps
The blush and coy on thy tender cheeks,
Is all forever mine.
Pretty lily sends beguiling of love,
Up away it go in the above
Dissolve in angel's deepest hearts,
Like Rappel's painted arts.

Why Parted Thee So Early

Fluttering within my heart,
Whispers of thy sweet love
A flower, crushed too- soon
Dousing me in flames
Leaving my soul shattered,

Why parted thee so early?
Thy kiss lies cold upon me,
Unlike a child's wavering dream
Etched forever into my senses
Time wipes memory it's said,
But it eases not my anguish
Why parted thee so early?
Love spilt over my soul,
Amidst those maudlin days
Thee, forever beautiful
My heart's true song
Whose tender lips I still long for.....
Why parted thee so early?

A song

Sing thou charm bird,
The sky is high
And beauty in it lie.
Sing thou fisherman,
The sea is full of charm
And believe it shall not harm.
Sing thou sweet bee,
Delight in the fragrance feel,
And she shall not allow thee to steal.
Sing thou dreading man,
Earth is paradise of beauty,
And protect it, our duty.

To Femi

Once our eyes spoke,
Language that's so sweet
Incessant passion and love
When our lips meet.
The anguish of our love,
Severed my heart
I write these lines,
I craft my art.
The moon in the bower,
Smiling at me
Mellowed in that light
I write for thee.
My heart broken a thousand pieces,
Swoon to death
I imbibe thy spirit
To listen to thy tender breath.

An Ode on Beauty

She was beauty's dearest daughter,
Eloquent and radiant in spirit
Like the charmed river's water
Flows thy beauty.
The lulled wind that dreams,
Endeavour in soft emotion
Like the moon that beams,
Gleams thy tender looks.
The red blossom love,
Can taste love's first kiss
My love, I love you
But forever.

Sweetly in the Fields

The skies so early,
The birds sing rarely
A girl I spy quite fairly.
Standing near her grazing lambs.
Hands clutching sweet lavender,
Lips of blood red shimmer
But for her deepening blush
Like a picture frozen in time.
On the flowing meadows green,
So coy and gently as ever seen
The girl in her early teens
So eloquent in her silence.

Tearfully We Two Part

Tearfully we two part,
In the dying light
Of the fading night
With kisses four in number
That is hardly for me to recollect
The girl, I loved so much,
Is a history now
My pain i can't tell
My emotion I can't court
But the effusion that springs
Deep in my heart's core
Is love for thee
So please do come back,
Come back to me
Those sweet kisses we made
On that last hour
Of the fading night
Is the sweetest memorial,
I can remember later in my life.

Love at First Sight

She shined upon me like a diamond,
So beauteous to see
Mellowed in the glow of light
She is like a flowing dove,
Whose waters sprinkle as love.
I court the music,
The sweet rhythm of passion
Flows like a rapture in me
Has the magical reflection,
Of our love at first sight.
I think the sweetest vision man can gain,
Is the love at first sight
It's beam of light
Has sparkled our glances,
For a moment's joy.

On The Death of a Beloved

Thy kiss from lips expire,
 Thou died in tender youth
Blood with all its fire
Burns deep in me
Thee like a flower crushed
Bearing the pain and sorrow
Swells terribly in my soul,
My heart has been half broken
Severely suffering it's pain
Loss of a beloved reflects in my eyes
Our days made for loving
The cool breezy night was our time
Madness and sweetness we delighted
In the light of the moon

Thy rosy tinge on where i kissed
But those gentle kisses are only memories
I still long to taste thy lips....
" In memory thou live,
And in memory thou fade"
A gentle passionate word to thee,
I love you too death.

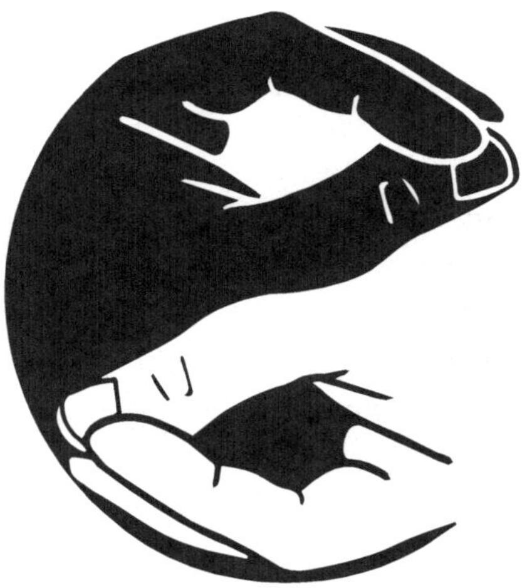

Silence

Those eyes art closed,
Those ears art never hearing
Death triumphed and life failed.
The body where the soul has left,
Lies in the burial chamber
And some one for him weep.

View from a Hill

Early dawn's grace falls,
Brightly shading the sky's hue
I see beauty's soft shower in Mary
With her eyes of compassionate blue
Standing eloquently in the green
Sweet musical echo from the waters,
Awakening chirping insects

Soft rhymes in the blowing breeze
Swelling through bird's breasts
The peasant girls with blushing cheeks
The crystal clear gushing stream
Doubled my tender heart's pleasure
Then I saw marching troops

Severing human heads with their swords
The fallen soldiers heads were also chopped off,
Blooding the soil,
The sight lies me in tears
The voices of so many dying men
Deeply anguished my vision

The sight vexes my pulsating heart,
Some corpses given to vultures
Sons of victory tuning the harp's string
Sons of victory making a river of blood
Today i witnessed
Both peace and destruction.

I sing a Song

I sing a song,
Deep in my heart
That has found an echo
In the heart of a girl.
The music that she bears,
Is tender and sweet
Mellowed in the glow of love
Thus so soft in emotion.
Long, long after
When I meet thee
Will you sing me that song?
The vow of our love.

Love's First Sweetness

It was love I knew,
Rhyming from my pen,
Praising a girl
Whom I met up in the glen.
I saw Heaven's glow on her cheeks,
With a sweet blush
She covering her beauty's coy
But love in my heart terribly gush.
I dream of lying down on her lap,
Above spying her ripening breast
Life floating in sweetness,
Or would be in a dream or rest?

My Last Love Letter

The brush of romance,
Last drop of human tear
Sealed with a magical lust
My last love letter
Only for thee.
Days of my youth,
Is still blooming
Darkening within my soul
Simple letter I carve,
For thy loving.
The dying flower of love,
Withering away with time
Reflects in my letter
Yet I write
For thy remembrance.
Can time teach us love?
A fallen heart,
A failed emotion
A sunken soul
But how deep in love still...

love

O Beautiful Lady, O Beautiful Lady

O beautiful lady, O beautiful lady,
How young is my sweet love
Fluttering like a full born rose
And flowing like a crystal clear dove.
Thy moan is so eloquent to my ears,
Overflowing like a strain of melodious note
Soften in blooming love
Gently it bears in my heart.
Those frozen lips,
Those looks that I long to cherish
My love for thee is wild
Can my love for thee be scarce? No.

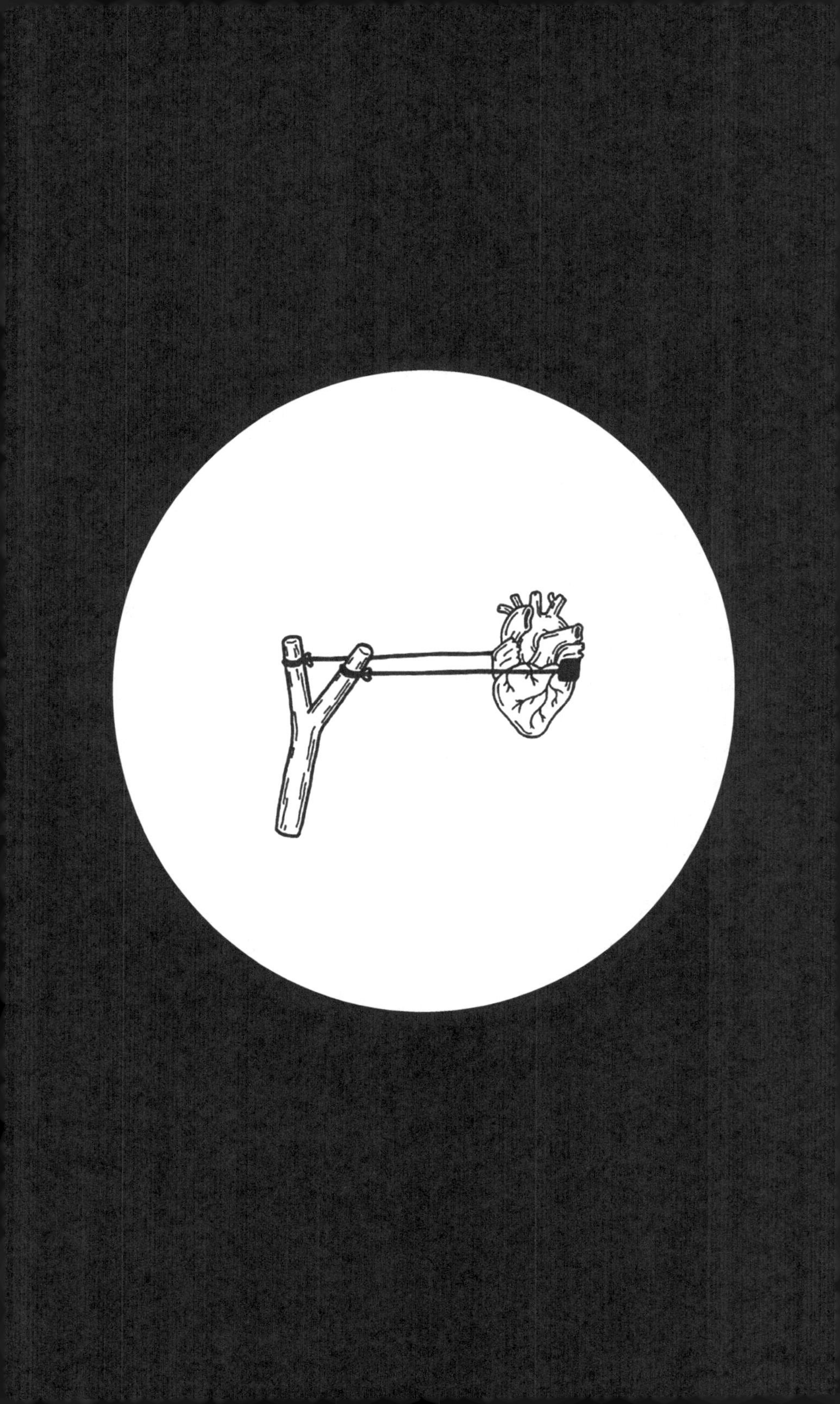

She Left Me

She left me,
Gone forever
Into the silent darkness
Like a beautiful song
That's over
T'was once sung
From my heart
T'was our song of love
The tender bushes,
Have withered away
And those parted lips
Where once I imprinted
My gentle kisses
Today lies frozen
With cold,
O my love is frozen like snow.

Forget Me Not, O Dona

The thirst of bloodlust love,
Silence of innocent heart
Stained tear drops in the soul
Burial chamber and dead hopes
How can I relinquish my sweet love?
But "forget me not", O Dona.
The last kiss of love,
Has expired from my lips
T'was like a parting kiss
Now an anguished memory
Forever within me,
But " forget me not" , O Dona.
Where are the flowers of love?
My love where art thou?
How deep in love am I,
Our glory once foretold
Silence and tears
But " forget me not", O Dona.

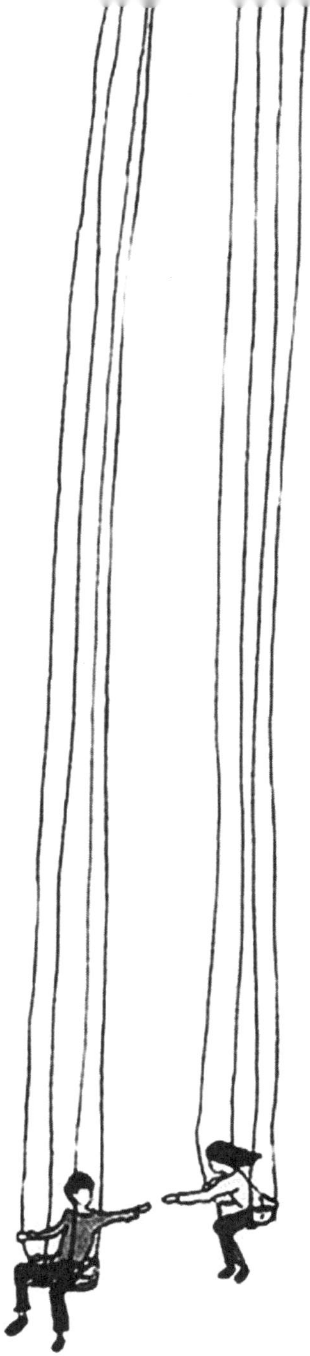

O Beautiful Caroline, My Parting Love

Sweet girl, like a blooming rose
With full of dewy wine
Outpours the tender love
Cherished in a soft heart
Burns in my dancing blood.
How sweeter was thy kiss?
That I will miss
Thy dear name
Shall remain in me
Can I forget thee? No.
I fly to a distant land,
With memories of our parting love
Yet behold within my breast
A new place for me to rove
But shall I find my love?
As the years will flow by,
If we meet again
My sweet girl
How should I greet thee?
With kisses.

A Lament

This heart may pause to breathe,
Bard of passion and fool
The end of life is death
To take a long slumber.
My heart is not green,
Nor in my wretched soul
The flowers of love are dead
Reviving passions and all.
There may be a few to grieve,
Over my untimely departure
I lived my live in deception
Of love and irresistible desires.
For this epitaph is truly yours,
On whose shell lies the last kiss
In honourable death for this boy,
Grief over my loss, you will miss.

Ode To Emlyn

Thee arises in my pensive dreams,
Gleams before my vision,
Language that is so sweet,
Earthly beauty's shower.
I still long to taste thy lips,
A beauty that made thy slave
Glittering glances
Attached me to thee forever.
The smiling flowers of love,
That blossoms in my heart
Is for thee
My dearest girl.
Farewell, the very word,
Brings me thoughts of anguish
Pain and tears,
I love you forever.

To Music

How sweet the echo flows?
From the voice of the nightingale,
Seated happily in a branch
Singing melodiously
In the light of the moon.

I listen to thy song,
Carry me into ecstasy
Comes the flood of joy
The enchanting of music,
Springs in my heart's core.

O sweet bird,
Sing me a love song
In which my heart should sink
Give me the inspiration,
To pen my next poem.

Longing

O beautiful girl, I depart this land
Ne'er to return again
Ne'er to hold thy hand
Ne'er can I listen thy musical strain.
I dream of returning to thee,
For one last kiss
Let me say my farewell
To thou, my dearest.

Time ceased our sweet love,
I hear thy voice
Still inside my soul
For me to rejoice.

I leave thee behind,
But still thou holds my heart
What sweet thoughts can wipe,
The gloom inside me.
My world only thou knew,
What is life's greatest blessing
Without thee
I'm broken forever.

Dew Drops

Tender dew drops falls from the sky,
Gently touches my love's eye
Sparkles with her blush
Like mellowed to my vision.

The glow of the morn,
Reflects in her beauty
Radiant in spirit
Sweet in her youth.

She twinkles like the star,
With eyes covering the coy
Singing a blissful air
In sweet throat.

Ode to the Sleeping Beauty

O midnight's dreaming girl,
Wake O, wake from thy slumber
Thy love is waiting for thee,
Chanting a tuneless number.

How soft, how eloquent
Remains thy beauty today
Like the stars that gently shine,
In the celestial milky way.

Awake, arise my dear love,
Let me gaze at thy eyes
Thy looks truly glowing
Radiant and sweet.

Lines Addressed to a Childhood Sweetheart

On the barren fields,
Where once my sweetheart roamed
Springs no myrtle today.

Now a shudder comes,
It covers my soul
I see gloom casts over me.

My childhood sweet is gone,
She is gone forever
Gone into the silence of the night.

Anguished whimpers upon my ears,
Reflects my silent deep tears
The sign of my pain.
I will ne'er know where she is gone,
But yet I'm sure
She will ne'er return back.

The fever of love,
Dwells in my deep soul
Tearfully I remember our moments.